Tropical Fish

Loren P. Woods

Curator of Fishes
Field Museum of Natural History
Chicago, Illinois

Illustrated by Kyuzo Tsugami

Follett Publishing Company Chicago

ISBN 0 695-40175-0 Titan binding
ISBN 0 695-80175-9 Trade binding
Library of Congress Catalog Card Number: 74-118956
First Printing

People have kept small and colorful fishes in shallow pools or bowls since ancient times. The Chinese and Japanese raised fancy goldfish. They chose only the most colorful fishes to be parents, so that their children would be colorful, too. This is called SELECTIVE BREEDING. The Siamese developed fancy fighting bettas by selective breeding. Ancient Romans kept red mullets in pools. Guests could admire the fish and select ones to be eaten.

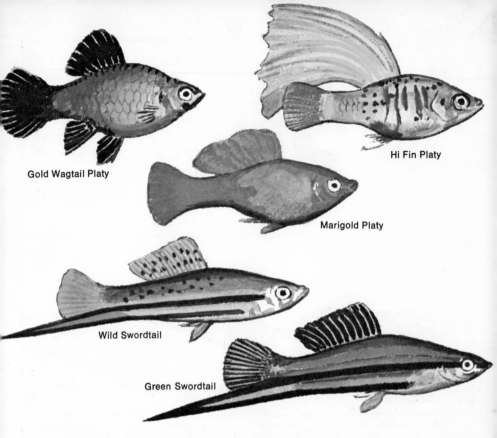

Gold Wagtail Platy

Hi Fin Platy

Marigold Platy

Wild Swordtail

Green Swordtail

Recently, many people have tried to improve the appearance of different kinds of tropical fishes. They use selective breeding and LINE BREEDING. Fishes used as parents for line breeding should be no more closely related than first cousins.

Many new varieties, or STRAINS, of several types of fishes have been produced by line breeding. This is how colorful green swordtails and guppies were obtained from less colorful parents.

5

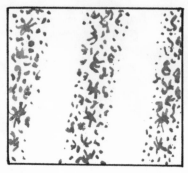

Color cells with
pigment contracted

Color cells with
pigment expanded

Color cells group together
to make different patterns

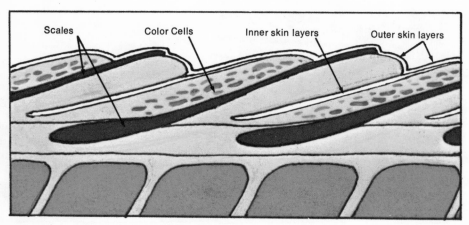

Cross-section showing fish's skin, scales, and color cells

Colors and markings on fishes are made by color cells.
These cells are too small to be seen without the help of a
microscope. Each color cell contains pigment of only one
color. Different color cells may be close together
or overlapping.

6

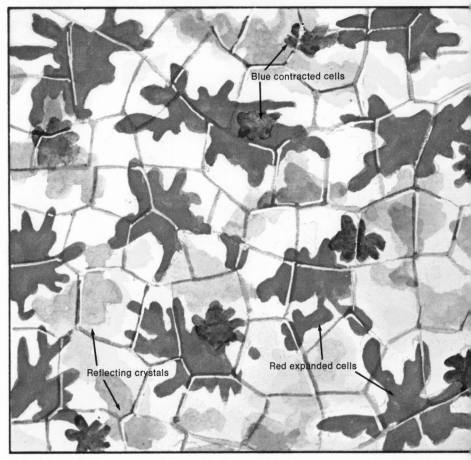

If the blue cells contract and the red cells expand, the outer covering of the fish will be red.

Some color cells may also contain reflecting crystals. These crystals produce IRRIDESCENCE. This means that they reflect rainbow-colored light.

Colors help fishes to recognize each other. Colors also tell the fish's mood and whether it is healthy.

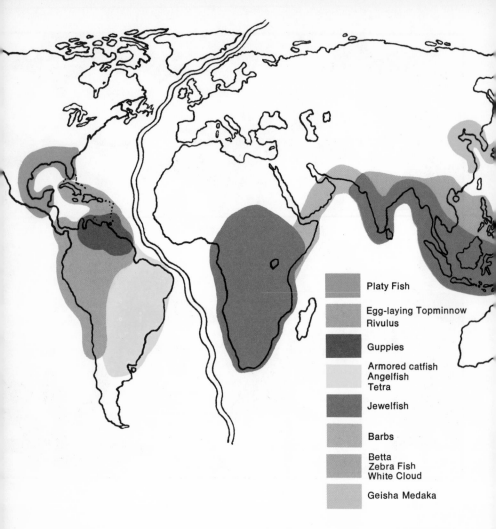

Platy Fish

Egg-laying Topminnow
Rivulus

Guppies

Armored catfish
Angelfish
Tetra

Jewelfish

Barbs

Betta
Zebra Fish
White Cloud

Geisha Medaka

Today, hundreds of kinds of tropical fishes can be kept in fish tanks, or aquariums. Fishes that are small, lively, and brightly colored are the best ones to keep. The map shows areas of the world where the most popular kinds of tropical fishes live.

8

If you would like to be an aquarist and keep tropical fishes, there are some things you should think about. Where are you going to put your tank or tanks? Tropical fishes should be in a well-lit part of the room. An even temperature, during the day and the night, is important. This means that your aquarium should not be in direct sunlight, close to a radiator or a cool breeze.

The filter and air pump help to keep a large aquarium clean.

Plants

Air Pump

Thermometer

Heater

Filter

You can begin by using a glass jar or a bowl for your aquarium. All aquariums should have covers that easily allow the light through. You can quickly learn the habits and needs of tropical fishes if you have only one kind in each aquarium or tank.

Larger tanks with several kinds of fresh-water fishes or salt-water fishes are fun to keep. But first, it is important to learn how to care for the fishes.

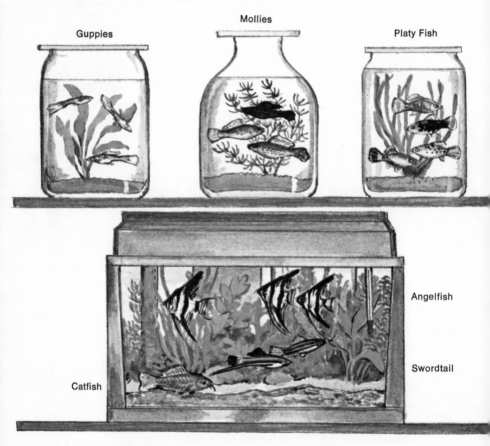

Guppies

Mollies

Platy Fish

Angelfish

Swordtail

Catfish

A large tank requires more equipment than the smaller tanks.

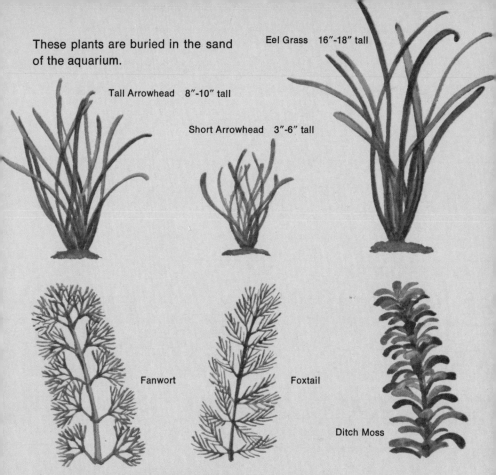

These plants are buried in the sand of the aquarium.

Eel Grass   16"-18" tall

Tall Arrowhead   8"-10" tall

Short Arrowhead   3"-6" tall

Fanwort

Foxtail

Ditch Moss

These plants can be buried in the sand or allowed to float freely.

One kind of fish and one kind of plant in a small tank is best. In a large tank, a variety of plants can be used. A combination of short, tall, fine-leaved, and broad-leaved plants makes the tank look pretty. Plants and rocks provide a place for fishes to rest, hide, or lay their eggs.

11

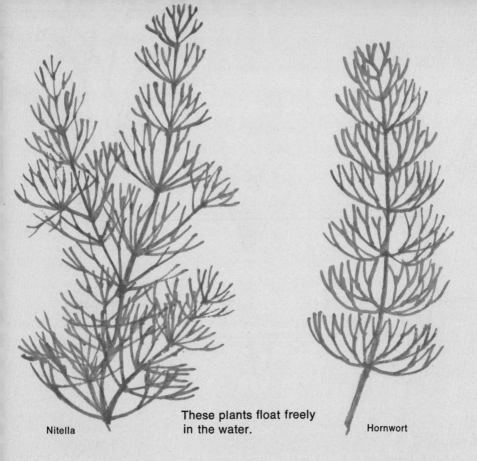

Nitella

These plants float freely in the water.

Hornwort

Tropical fishes can be kept in water without plants or with artificial plants made of plastic. Real plants are best in an aquarium because some fishes use them for food and shelter. Plants that float freely in the water are good egg-catchers and provide a good place for the baby fishes to hide. The shade made by aquarium plants will help slow the growth of algae. Algae are the unwanted green films on the walls of the tank.

Carefully place a sick or injured fish in a small jar
filled with water from the aquarium the fish lived
in before.

Many tropical fishes live for only a few months; others
live for a few years. They will stay healthy in aquariums if
they have good food, proper water temperature, and plenty
of room to swim around. A sick or injured fish should be
separated from the others. It should be kept in a tank by
itself while it recovers.

If you get new fishes or new plants, be sure to keep them
in separate tanks for a few days. Open the new bunches of
plants and wash them with water. This will help
keep your fishes healthy.

Different topminnows can be raised in aquariums. They are small fishes that prefer food that floats on top of the water.

Most topminnows have scales on their heads. All of them have teeth in their jaws. Those that lay eggs are called EGG LAYERS. Those that have their young alive are called LIVE BEARERS.

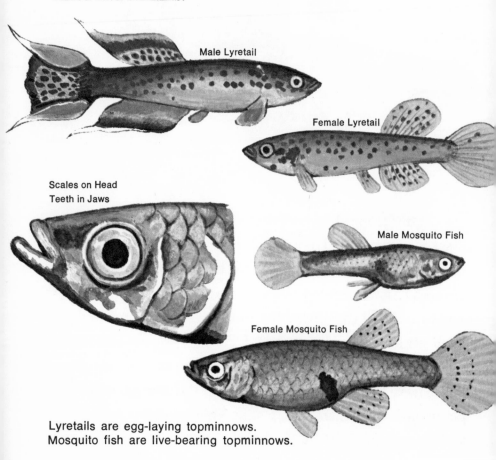

Male Lyretail

Female Lyretail

Scales on Head
Teeth in Jaws

Male Mosquito Fish

Female Mosquito Fish

Lyretails are egg-laying topminnows.
Mosquito fish are live-bearing topminnows.

14

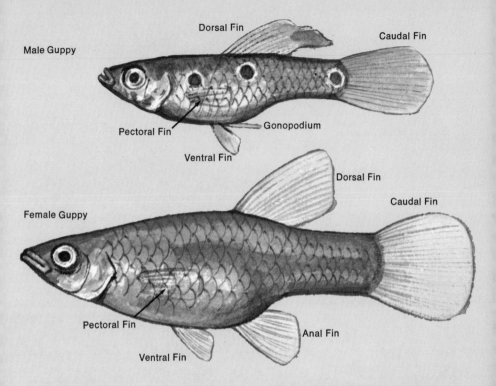

Male Guppy

Dorsal Fin

Caudal Fin

Pectoral Fin

Gonopodium

Ventral Fin

Female Guppy

Dorsal Fin

Caudal Fin

Pectoral Fin

Anal Fin

Ventral Fin

An adult male guppy is only about one inch long, but an adult female guppy is about one and one-half inches long. The gonopodium of the male guppy is used to fertilize the eggs in the female guppy.

Guppies are live-bearing topminnows. They are very easy to keep. This makes them a good fish for your first aquarium. A guppy swims with quick sideway movements of its tail fin. The back fin and side fins are used for turning and stopping. The male guppies seem to chase the female guppies constantly. Once in a while a male will nip another male, but they are usually peaceful.

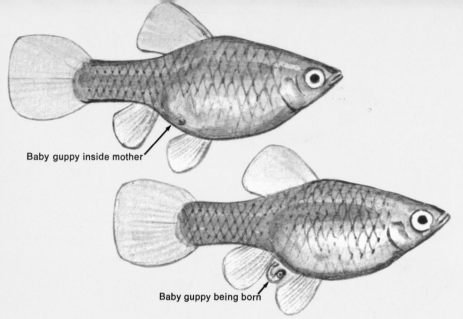

Baby guppy inside mother

Baby guppy being born

Baby guppies swimming and hiding in plants

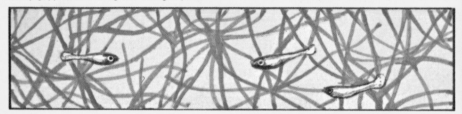

The eggs of guppies are kept inside the mother, where they are fertilized by the father. The young are born when they are ready to swim. The mother guppy will bear from 6 to more than 60 young at one time. The young are usually born at night. They grow rapidly and can have young of their own in 3 or 4 months. A mother guppy can produce a new family, or BROOD, every 4 to 6 weeks, if she is well fed and kept warm in water that is 72° F.

As a guppy breeder, you can get a father guppy to produce sons much like himself. To do this, you must mate him with his mother or his sister. This is called INBREEDING. A guppy breeder can inbreed his guppies to obtain more of one fancy kind of guppy.

Guppy breeders need many small aquariums. A fancy male guppy is kept in a tank by himself until a special female is chosen for mating. Each fancy young guppy may be kept separate until the breeder decides how he will mate them.

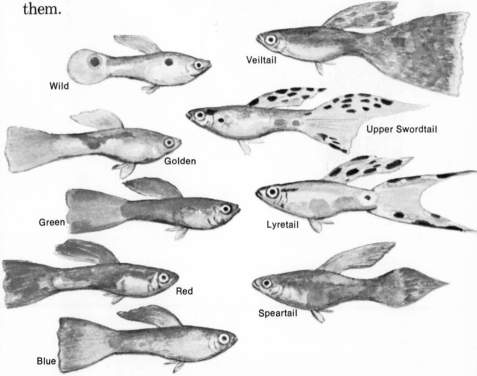

Veiltail

Wild

Upper Swordtail

Golden

Green

Lyretail

Red

Speartail

Blue

Breeders have developed different kinds of guppies by using a male wild guppy as a parent. Male wild guppies are never alike in color or shape and size of fins. These are some kinds that breeders have developed. 17

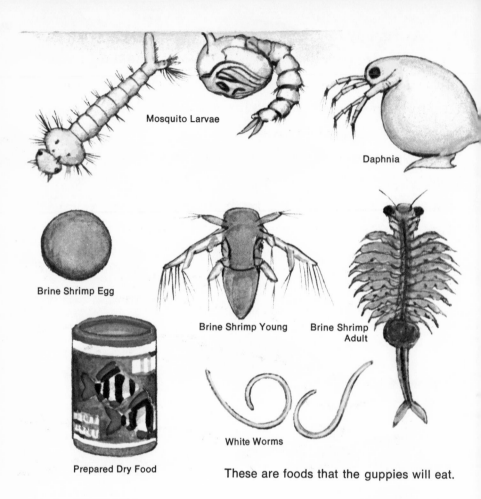

Mosquito Larvae

Daphnia

Brine Shrimp Egg

Brine Shrimp Young

Brine Shrimp Adult

Prepared Dry Food

White Worms

These are foods that the guppies will eat.

Guppies eat many different foods. Live food, such as daphnia, mosquito larvae, and brine shrimp, is good for them. This food can live in the tank with the guppies and will be available whenever the baby fish are hungry. White worms, shrimp meal, and prepared dry foods are also good. Almost any high protein food that is finely cut can be used.

Black

Golden

Red

Blacktailed Red

Speckled

Blue

Many colorful platy fish have been developed by selective breeding. Platy fish are easy to care for in an aquarium.

Wild

Although platy fish are a little larger than guppies, they are live-bearing topminnows, also. After just one mating, a mother platy can produce a brood about every 4 weeks.

Platy fish are very active. They swim at the top, on the bottom, and in the midwater. These topminnows like to nibble on algae, and they will eat live or prepared dry foods. They should be in temperatures ranging from 70° F. to 80° F. If 1 teaspoon of salt is added per 2 gallons of water, the platy fish will do better.

Other live-bearing topminnows are mollies and swordtails. Swordtails will grow to 5 inches in length, but they start producing young when they are only two inches long. A mother swordtail may have 6 broods every 5 to 9 weeks. There can be as many as 150 young per brood, but usually the number is smaller.

Black mollies mate less often than swordtails and platy fish. They like to nibble on green algae. And like platy fish, they do better with a little salt in their water.

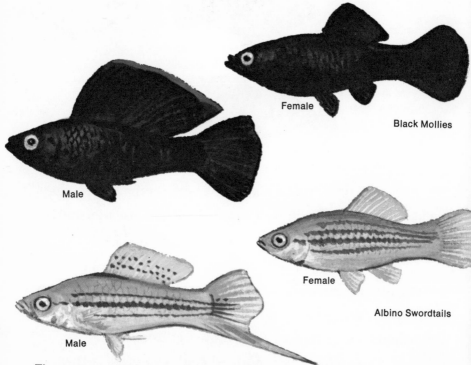

Female

Black Mollies

Male

Female

Albino Swordtails

Male

There are many kinds of mollies and swordtails. Mollies are usually three inches long and smaller than swordtails.

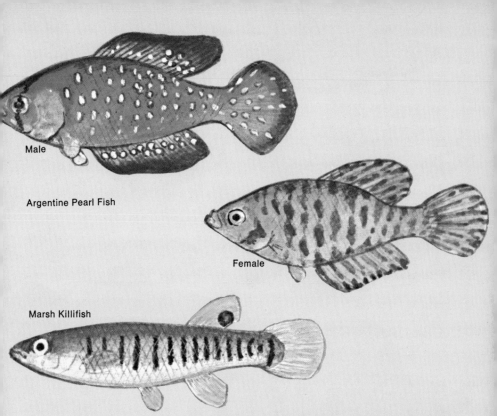

Male

Argentine Pearl Fish

Female

Marsh Killifish

Argentine pearl fish and marsh killifish are about three inches long when fully grown. A female marsh killifish lays her eggs on peat moss on the bottom of a pool. Breeders are able to transport marsh killifish eggs easily by placing the dried peat moss in plastic containers. Then they can place the peat moss in water, and in about half an hour tiny killifish will begin to swim around.

There are also different kinds of egg-laying topminnows, such as the Argentine pearl fish, marsh killifish, lyretail, geisha medaka, and rivulus. Some lay their sticky eggs on floating plants; others lay their eggs on the bottom of a pool or stream.

21

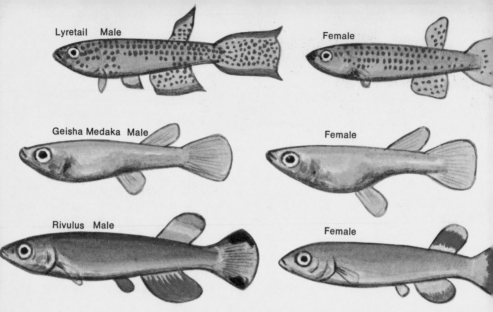

Adult lyretails and geisha medakas are about two inches long. An adult rivulus is about two and one-half inches long.

Lyretails live in tropical waters of western Africa. In an aquarium lyretails will lay their eggs, or spawn, on a special spawning mop made of nylon yarn. Aquarists all over the world trade and ship the eggs.

Geisha medakas come from Japan, Korea, and China. They can live in temperatures ranging from 32° F. to 90° F. Their eggshells are easy to see into and are used to study the development of the fish in the living egg.

Many kinds of rivuluses live in the West Indies and Central and South America. A golden or green rivulus will lay 1 egg a day for several weeks. Their eggs hatch after 2 weeks.

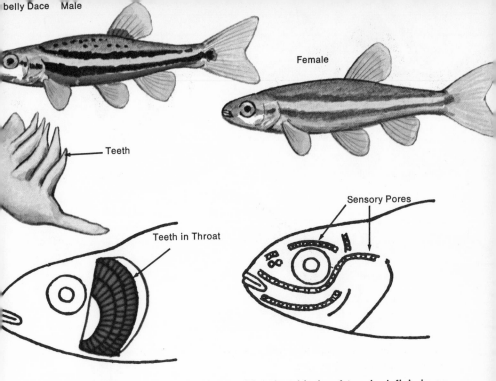

Female

Teeth

Teeth in Throat

Sensory Pores

Redbelly daces should not be kept with other kinds of tropical fish in an aquarium.

True minnows are a different group of small fishes. They have no scales on their heads, as topminnows do. But some true minnows have horny growths on their heads at egg-laying time. A topminnow's teeth are located in its jaws, but a true minnow's teeth are in its throat.

Redbelly daces are true minnows. They live in cool, clear creeks. They like lots of room in an aquarium and should not be kept with other fishes. Their water should not be warmer than 72° F.

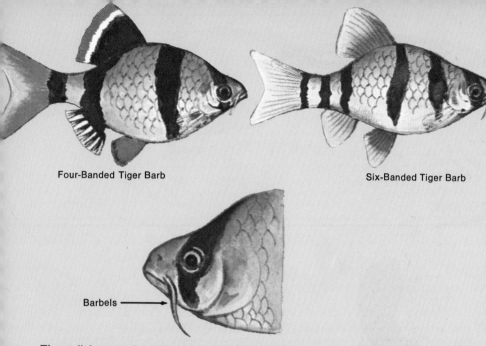

Four-Banded Tiger Barb

Six-Banded Tiger Barb

Barbels

These fish come from Sumatra and Borneo. They are usually about two or three inches long when full grown.

Some true minnows live in temperate and tropical climates around the world, except South America and Australia. Most kinds can be kept in aquariums. Tiger barbs, zebra fish, harlequins, and white clouds are favorites because of their small size and bright colors. They attract attention because they are constantly on the move.

A tiger barb has long feelers called barbels at the corners of its mouth. Tiger barbs eat algae and other food. Their aquarium should have good light so that the algae grow well.

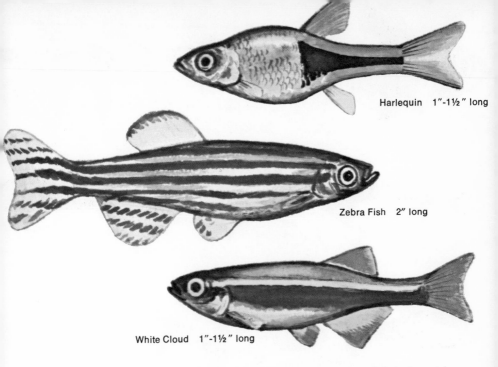

Harlequin 1"–1½" long

Zebra Fish 2" long

White Cloud 1"–1½" long

The harlequin fish is found in Sumatra and Malaya. The zebra fish is found in India. The white clouds are named after White Cloud Mountain in China.

Zebra fish spawn over a bare surface. Their eggs fall to the bottom and do not stick to anything.

The harlequin fish does not scatter its eggs, but hangs them on the underside of a leaf.

White clouds are very hardy and can stand temperatures from 40° F. to 90° F. They do best in water that is 70° F. A Chinese Boy Scout named Tan discovered these fish. White clouds should be well fed or they will eat their own eggs that are sticking on plants or the bottom of the aquarium.

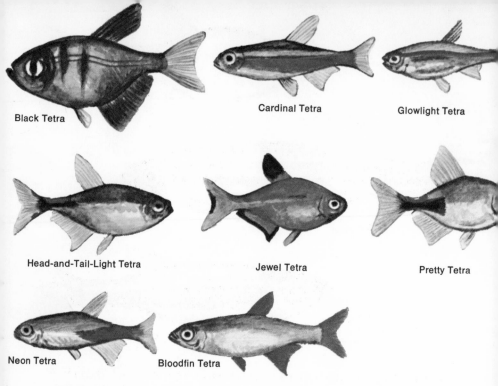

Black Tetra

Cardinal Tetra

Glowlight Tetra

Head-and-Tail-Light Tetra

Jewel Tetra

Pretty Tetra

Neon Tetra

Bloodfin Tetra

Tetras are also called tets. Adult tetras are one and one-half inches to two inches long.

Tetras are small, brilliantly colored fishes found in South America. There are many kinds of tetras. Some look like minnows, but tetras have teeth in their jaws. Many have an adipose fin. All tetras lay eggs, which stick to plants. Parents should be removed after spawning or they will eat the eggs.

Several kinds of tetras can be kept in the same tank. They eat almost every type of food. They are always lively, swimming in all parts of the tank. They move with a quick flick of the tail fin or their other fins.

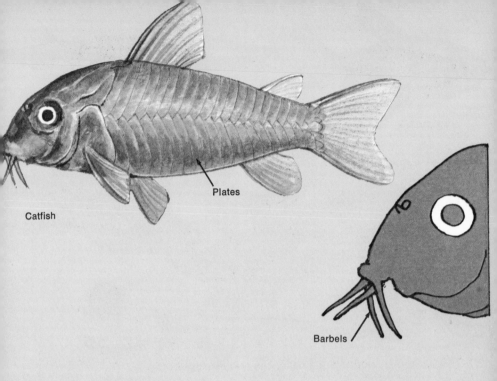

Catfish

Plates

Barbels

This catfish is found in South America and is two to three inches long.

Catfishes do not have true scales, but some are covered with bony plates. They have broad, flat heads and whiskers. They can taste things with lower parts of their head, whiskers, and lips. All female catfishes lay eggs.

Like minnows and tetras, there are many kinds of catfishes. Usually one or two are kept in an aquarium and help keep it clean by eating the bits of dirt and trash on the bottom. They should be fed other food, also. Small armored catfishes are the ones most often kept in an aquarium.

27

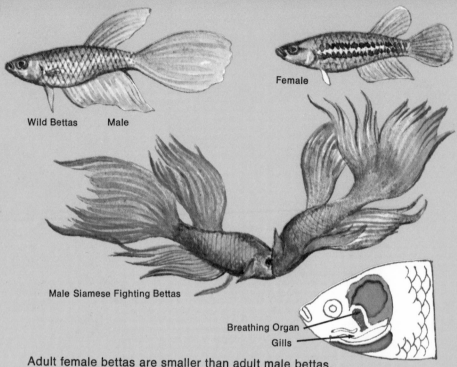

Wild Bettas   Male

Female

Male Siamese Fighting Bettas

Breathing Organ

Gills

Adult female bettas are smaller than adult male bettas.

Bettas have been selected and mated by aquarists for more than one hundred years. Wild bettas are smaller than those raised in aquariums. Several wild kinds have been crossed, but none are as colorful as the Siamese fighting bettas. They bite or tear each other's fins when they fight. Their damaged fins grow back quickly.

A betta breathes by using air held in a chamber on each side of its head above the gills. Blood is very near the thin skin of these chambers and takes in oxygen from the air. The fish makes quick trips to the surface to get rid of the used air bubble in its mouth and take in a new one.

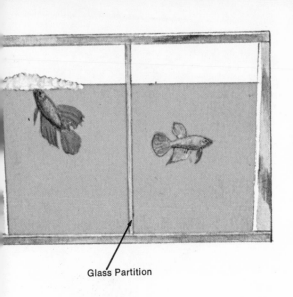

Glass Partition

s partition can be used to separate the mother betta from the father betta
he prepares the nest. This father betta is picking up the young. He guards
ung or eggs and often blows more bubbles to keep the nest large enough.

When bettas are ready to spawn, the father builds a
nest of bubbles. The mother has to be kept away until the
nest is ready or the father will chase her. As she lays eggs, he
picks them up in his mouth and blows them into the nest.
The mother should be removed when she finishes laying eggs.
After a few days the eggs will hatch. The father should be
removed when the young leave the nest and start swimming
upward to get air. The swimming young can be placed in
small containers for individual feeding.

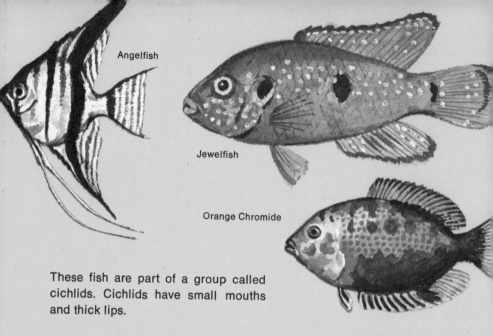

Angelfish

Jewelfish

Orange Chromide

These fish are part of a group called cichlids. Cichlids have small mouths and thick lips.

Angelfish from South America are beautiful. They swim slowly and use their pectoral fins alternately. They lay their eggs in rows on a leaf or stem. When the babies hatch, the parents fasten them to another leaf or stem. Each baby is stuck there for several days by a sticky spot on its head. This keeps the babies in one place, so the parents can look after them.

The jewelfish from Africa and the orange chromide from India are relatives of the angelfish. Jewelfishes should be kept in an aquarium by themselves because they chase other fishes.

By selecting tropical fish that interest you, your aquarium can prove to be an enjoyable hobby.

Words Younger Children May Need Help With
(Numbers refer to page on which the word first appears)

4 bettas
  mullet
5 swordtails
  guppies
  platy
6 pigment
7 irridescence
  reflecting crystals
8 mollie
  topminnow
  rivulus
  tetra
  angelfish
  barbs
  jewelfish
  geisha medaka
  zebra fish

9 aquarist
  radiator
  thermometer
11 fanwort
12 nitella
  hornwort
  artificial
  algae
13 lyretail
15 caudal
  dorsal
  ventral
  pectoral
  gonopodium
18 mosquito larvae
  daphnia
  brine shrimp

24 harlequin
  barbels
30 chromide
  cichlids

THINGS YOU CAN DO

Raise your own tropical fish. Before selecting fish, you will need equipment that will help keep your tropical fish in good condition. A small tank with a 2 or 5 gallon water capacity is needed. Also, it is important to have a glass cover for keeping out dust and dirt, preventing water evaporation, and keeping fish from jumping out of the tank. Special lights, heaters, air pumps, and filters are not necessary in the beginning. They do help keep very delicate fish in good condition, but you can have much fun without the added accessories. However, a soft mesh net, algae scraper, and floating thermometer are useful accessories. Also, inexpensive storage boxes that are 10″ x 14″ x 6″ can be purchased from the variety store and used for holding your fish while cleaning or repleting the tank, isolating sick fish, isolating spawning pairs, raising small fry, or hatching brine shrimp eggs.

Raise infusoria and hatch brine shrimp eggs. You can buy infusoria at the pet store and then place them in a container filled with pond water. Place the container in a sunny area. When the water is green, you can feed the infusoria to young fry. Buy dried brine shrimp eggs and put them in a gallon of water that contains 6 tablespoons of salt. Young fishes can be fed the newly hatched brine shrimp, too.

Raise snails in your aquarium. Snails can be interesting to watch in your aquarium. They are helpful because they eat algae and uneaten fish food. However, snails tend to overpopulate very easily, so they must be carefully watched.

Learn how to breed tropical fish. If you have live-bearing fish, be sure there is plenty of floating plants for the young fry to hide in. Remember to remove the parents of the young fry after they are born. If you have egg-laying fish, separate the male and female until the female appears to be swollen with eggs. Then return the male to the tank the female is in and wait for the pair to spawn. The male and female should be separated from the newly laid eggs, since some egg-laying fish eat the eggs. However, this is not true of all tropical fish.